Enjoying Equal House, Why One of the Oldest Astrological House Systems is so Easy to Use

Mary English

Published by Future Path Publishing, 2023.

While every precaution has been taken in the preparation of this book, the publisher assumes no responsibility for errors or omissions, or for damages resulting from the use of the information contained herein.

ENJOYING EQUAL HOUSE, WHY ONE OF THE OLDEST ASTROLOGICAL HOUSE SYSTEMS IS SO EASY TO USE

First edition. April 12, 2023.

Copyright © 2023 Mary English.

ISBN: 979-8215678138

Written by Mary English.

Also by Mary English

The Astrology of Lovers, How Astrology Can Help You Love Better
The Astrology of Indigos, Everyday Solutions to Spiritual Difficulties
Neptune in Pisces, An Astrological Search for Enlightenment
Enjoying Equal House, Why One of the Oldest Astrological House Systems is so Easy to Use

Watch for more at https://www.maryenglish.com.

Table of Contents

Introduction 1

History of Equal House | Level One: Beginner 5

Why Using Equal House is Easy to Understand & Remember 27

House Meanings & Keywords 45

Chart Examples 51

Empty Houses and Sign & House Rulers | Level Two: Intermediate 61

Chart Rulers | Level Three: Advanced 73

Exercises 89

This book is dedicated to my

youngest sister

Katherine, Francis English

"You Are and Were, My Best Ever Sister"

Enjoying Equal House
Why One of The Oldest Astrological House Systems is so Easy to Use.

Mary English

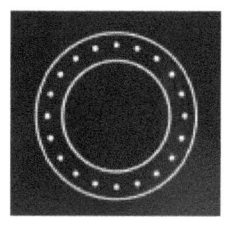

Future Path Publishing, Bath, U.K.

Copyright © 2023 Mary English

All rights reserved.

Contents

Acknowledgements

Introduction

Level One: Beginner

Chapter One : History of Equal House

Chapter Two : Why Using Equal House is Easiest to Understand & Remember

Chapter Three : House Meanings & Keywords

Chapter Four : Chart Examples

Level Two: Intermediate

Chapter Five : Empty Houses, Sign and House Rulers

Level Three: Advanced

Chapter Six: Chart Rulers

Chapter Seven : Exercises

Endnotes

Jargon Buster

References

Bibliography

Acknowledgements

I would like to thank the following people for their help and support with writing this book.

Deep thanks to Izzi Daly for the lovely cover Art https://www.instagram.com/izzkat.art/

Big hugs and thanks to Leah Wilt for the really helpful internal illustrations https://leahwilt.com/

First Class thank yous to Julie Lee for her first draft encouragement and ideas.

For taking the time to read through and feedback:

Diana Anderson,

Laura Boys,

Christine Cleere,

Leah Crispi,

Bobby Gribble,

Ms Amanda Leo,

Len Marlow,

Mrs Cathy McCormack

Dawn McKoy,

Sheila Steele

Jennifer Taylor,

Jill Trelease.

Big extra thanks to Sylvia Bishop for running the fab 'Writers with Faces' online writer's space.

Gratitude to Alois Treindl https://www.astro.com/people/treindl_e.htm[1] for owning/hosting/running the lovely Astrodienst website and allowing me to use the charts.

---

1. https://www.astro.com/people/treindl_e.htm

Introduction

This book is written to help you understand the very basics of Astrology without giving you a headache. Far too many books are written to confuse. This is not one of them.

However, I will make some assumptions.

I will assume you at least know what sign of the Zodiac you are and you've investigated various books, websites and/or podcasts to give you some understanding of how Astrology works and what it can and can't do.

In this book I am not teaching you *everything* about Astrology.

I'm helping you learn a *specific* house system.

And in my professional opinion based on over 25 years of work in this field, the Equal House System is the easiest to use and understand.

If you want to make Astrology complex, you certainly can. You can go deeper and deeper into the subject and learn complicated techniques.

You can spend hours calculating things and you might enjoy that.

I don't.

I'm of the opinion that simple is best.

Please excuse my use of the acronym: KISS

Keep it Simple Stupid

(I'm not implying that *you're* stupid though, far from it)

And once you've mastered the simple things you can choose what to do next.

I've found that Astrology works perfectly well at a simple level and can give insights and understanding to difficult situations, relationships and challenges.

Life is difficult enough already.

I've also made this book short and sweet.

You could easily read it in one sitting.

Afterwards you'll have a much better idea of why I use this system and why it's easy, *much* easier to use.

I have divided this book into three 'levels'.

Level One: Chapters One-Four are for Beginners, or those with a basic grasp of Astrology

Level Two: Chapter Five is Intermediate, taking Astrology a little further

Level Three: Chapters Six-Seven are more advanced, and take you to a deeper knowledge of possibility and uses.

For the purposes of this book I urge you to use the website I recommend called www.astro.com

Then you can follow-along with what I'm explaining for you.

Using the website is free.

Make an account with them and then you can store 100 charts on there for free.

If you *don't* make account with them, you won't be able to access some of the information I'm sharing with you.

And No, I'm not on commission!!

I hope this book delivers on my promise and that by the end of it, you'll have a much better understanding of Equal House and why it's so enjoyable! :)

Mary English, Bath 2023

Chapter One

History of Equal House
Level One: Beginner

If you ever want to see astrologers fight, then start a discussion on the 'best' house system to use.

Here's a typical astrology forum discussion:

Q. I had a general question as to which house system most people use? I usually use either placidus or koch. I have heard that placidus is better for analyzing personality/psychological traits, and koch is better for transit and progressions. Any thoughts?

A. I have heard the opposite—Placidus is the best for natal and transits/progressions and Koch for psychological.

In all of this discussion, there wasn't a single mention of one of the oldest systems.

The focus was on all the other systems: Placidus, Regiomontanus, Koch, Porphyry, Whole Sign and Campanus.

Not one person mentioned Equal House!

I've used the Equal House system since I first learned astrology and I love it sooooo much!

I've used the other systems. However, as I'm *very* interested in chart shape, the shape of the chart doesn't show up as well in those other systems.

For more info on chart shape go to my podcast numbers One to Three

https://astromary.libsyn.com/episode-one-0

https://astromary.libsyn.com/episode-two-0

https://astromary.libsyn.com/episode-three-0

Before I get into how this system works, who uses it, its history and how some astrologers were led to use the now more popular system of Placidus, I just want to clarify there is room in Astrology for every house system.

I just prefer Equal House.

What is a Birth Chart or Natal Chart?

A birth chart is a little map of the sky on the day and time you were born.

It starts at a thing called the Ascendant (or Rising sign) and is, if you imagine a clock-face, at the quarter to nine/8.45am position and is calculated by using the time/date and location of the person's birth.

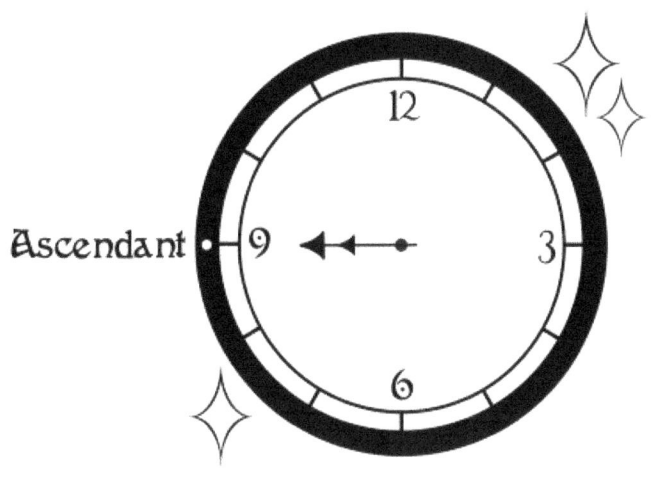

The Ascendant, the starting point of an Astro chart

An Astro chart can also be made for the 'beginning' of anything: the date a company was formed, an investment was made or when you move house or relocate.

The parts of the chart are called as follows:

The MC = Medium Coeli = Latin for "middle of sky" . Called the Midheaven, it is the highest point in the Sun's path everyday, approx 12pm (but not always, depends on time of year)

The IC = Imum Coeli = Latin for "bottom of sky" lies directly opposite

The Asc = Ascendant = from Latin ascendere (to ascend)

The DC = Descendant = from Latin descendere (to descend, go down)

House Systems

What is a house system?

An Astrological birth chart, or any horoscope chart, is divided up in some way to represent different areas of life.

Most modern charts are made as a circle, with the horizontal line across the chart representing the horizon. (Ancient charts were sometimes drawn as squares)

Anything below the horizon line would not be physically visible to us on Earth on the day of birth.

Anything above the line might be, depending on what planet is included as only seven are possible with the naked eye.

The three 'outer planets' : Uranus, Neptune and Pluto can only be seen with telescopes and hence were only discovered when telescopes were invented.

A chart can then be divided by signs, or by mathematical degrees.

This is where the arguments start.

But before I get to the arguments, I'd like to cover what houses are used for.

What Houses are Used For

The journey that the Sun makes 'around' the Earth in one year, is called the Ecliptic.

This circle around the Earth includes the path the Sun makes over our heads in one year.

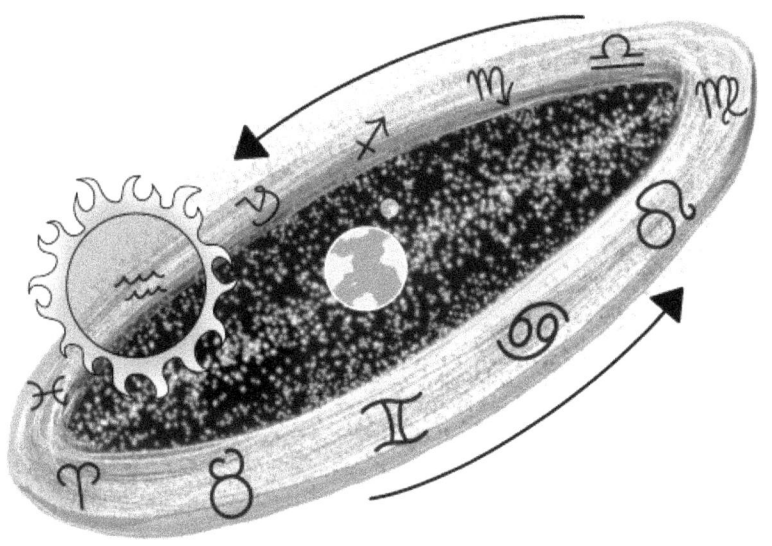

The Sun, the Earth and the Path the Sun Makes: Ecliptic

We know that the Sun doesn't actually travel around the Earth, it's the Earth that travels around the Sun.

However, in Astrology we calculate things from our perspective on Earth looking upwards at the sky and as you'll know, everyday the Sun rises and sets.

This path that the Sun makes around our heads has a belt of sky called the Zodiac, with the Ecliptic at its centre.

The Zodiac is a division of the sky along the ecliptic by the signs that you're familiar with: Aries-Pisces. They're calculated astronomically using the Spring Solstice as the first day of Aries.

A house system is a division of that circle by other methods, generally using some mathematical system or time system.

Having houses personalises the chart and gives each planet in it a 'home' hence the term house.

A bit like when you're sitting at a table with other people. Someone sitting right next to you is going to feel different to someone sitting at the opposite side of the table.

Any house system isn't real.

Unlike the planets and their orbits, it's not something that actually exists.

You could also say that the division of the Zodiac isn't 'real', however it does use astronomical calculations and is a precise method of measurement of the sky above our heads.

And there isn't a line in the sky between one sign and another!

Obviously our sky isn't divided into anything, let alone exact 30 degree segments. So we need to keep in mind that any house system is just a way of adding poetry and creativeness to the birth chart.

The Ephemeris

An Ephemeris is a written record that contains the plotting of each planet's motion through the sky everyday.

An Astrological ephemeris tells us what sign (part of the sky) each planet is in.

https://www.astro.com/swisseph/swepha_e.htm

You can find out what signs all the planets were in on the day you were born by using that Ephemeris, or a good computer programme or an online website like the one I recommend https://www.astro.com/

Be aware though that not all sites are accurate, and please don't rely completely on an astrology app.

Quite a lot of them are written by writers or coders NOT by Astrologers.

If you're lucky it will be.

Don't take the risk.

Make your chart on more than one website and see if anything changes.

If you want your chart to be perfectly accurate I always recommend the website https://www.astro.com/

Long may it exist, along with its wonderfully talented Pisces creator : Alois Treindl.

The information you will find might be something like this:

Maybe Sun in Virgo,

Moon in Aquarius,

Mercury in Libra..and so on.

Just that skimpy bit of information tells us quite a bit about the person or event.

Assuming this is a person we're talking about we could say:

Sun in Virgo:

They're concerned with specifics and enjoy perfection (although they may never attain it)

Moon in Aquarius:

Enjoys friendships to feel emotionally complete

Mercury in Libra:

Communicates in a polite, respectful manner, or loves to argue a point.

All well and good. This will help us 'understand' the person concerned quite well.

The problems arise when we need further detail about the person/company or event.

What's important for them?

Where are they happiest focusing their attention?

What values do they abide by and where do they 'shine' (this is discovered by the house location of the Sun)

Now, on the one hand houses aren't 'real' at all, so why all the bother about even constructing them?

Why not just list the planets and their signs and leave it at that?

Deeper Understanding

Well, Astrology hasn't left it at that and for over 2,000 years Astrologers have attempted to deepen their understanding of human-kind by proposing that not only do the signs the planets are in mean something, but so does their 'location' in the chart.

We then have to ask the valuable question: Why did *location* of planets become so important?

Astrology is a system.

Invented by humankind to 'make sense' of the world they were living in.

To begin with it was mostly observational.

Someone up a tower in Babylon called a ziggurat, looked up at the night sky.

While observing the night sky they then discovered that bits of what they saw moved each night.

The little bits of light (and not so little) seemed to move around their heads and be in different places...then return back to those same places.

They named these bits of light after various gods they were fond of.

Now considering that most people that you and I know, hardly even *look* up at the Moon on a regular basis, might know what the Sun looks like, but very *rarely* even consider, let alone look up at the sky at *night*, it makes you wonder what it was about the night sky that fascinated the Babylonians.

Either they had a lot of time on their hands, or more likely, they were curious beings and curiosity leads to understanding.

Which is good.

Their curiosity led them to eventually work out that those certain points of light moved, while the background of the stars didn't.

They didn't have telescopes or anything sophisticated.

Just beautiful clear night skies, something UK astrologers & astronomers only dream about...

They noted when the various points of light corresponded to crop failures or Kings being born or dying or wars starting.

Then a very complex system was built up to be able to predict when those same earthly thing happenings might happen again, based on what they've observed in the sky.

Genius.

We have to remember that Astrology has a very, very long history and came before Jesus and Christianity.

How do you think the those three wise men managed to locate where Jesus was located?

They probably followed Jupiter. According to some researchers the wise men who 'followed a star' could have followed the light of Jupiter. It hasn't been proven 100% but it's a fair idea.

Now, I can't pin point for you the exact date that houses started to be used.

P.G Maxwell-Stuart in his *Astrology From Ancient Babylon to the Present* says that a Latin poet called Marcus Manilus wrote a poem in five books called Astronomica approx AD30-40

"Book 3 discusses a subsidiary set of 'houses' relating to home, warfare, business, law, marriage, length of life, dangers, social class, children, character, health and success..." 1.

According to Nicholas Campion in his *The Dawn of Astrology*, houses started to be used in Hellenistic Astrology around 323 BC-31 BC

He also says:

"The meanings of the zodiac signs were worked out sometime between the fifth and first centuries BCE, perhaps in a gradual process, possibly in a series of innovative steps. What we do know is that, in the literature of

the first and second centuries CE, they are recognisably the same as in any modern text." 2.

How fantastic is that!

Those 'meanings' have hardly altered in over 2,000 years!

Boom!

We are using a system with a deep and rich history.

Wow!

A Short History of Equal House

Astrology was 'invented' by the Babylonians more than 2,000 years ago.

They made a correlation between the movement of the planets and life here on earth.

At first they only used it to predict wars, famines or floods and the use of astrology was confined to Kings.

It was much later that personal horoscopes for the general public were made.

Early examples of charts were made as squares, each square holding a name or symbol for each sign.

And some early astrologers calculated the position of the planets using a wonderful device called an Astrolabe.

These allowed users to quickly work out the Ascending sign, position of planets and signs of the Zodiac.

As sort of ancient app.

https://astromary.libsyn.com/episode-ninety-eight

I bought one from an elderly engineer who started making them in this retirement. Sadly he no longer makes them.

Mine hangs in pride of place on my office wall.

Reminding me that the system I use today was devised by some *very* clever people in the past.

https://astromary.libsyn.com/episode-120

Most Ancient System of All?

According to Colin Evans in *The New Waite's Compendium of Natal Astrology:*

> *The Equal House System (but with no use of the M.C. at all in olden days) is the most ancient system of all.* 3.

Up until the seventeenth century in England astrologers used Equal House.

Another old system called Porphyry divides the chart into four sections called quadrants. Using the Ascendant, Mid Heaven, IC and DC

Whole sign houses was a Hellinistic house system (but it wasn't called that then)

The Campanus and Regiomontanus systems are also other older systems that are still in use today.

(Don't ask me to explain them!)

The Placidus System

Then, in the eighteen century, the Placidus system took over.

Why was this?

A chap called Placidus de Tito was born in Italy in 1603. He was a monk and a professor of mathematics at the University of Padua. He died in 1688

The Placidus system named after him was actually 'invented' by the astronomer and mathematician Antonio Magini who first wrote about it in 1604 in Latin in his book

Tabulae primi mobilis, quas directionum vulgo dicunt, quibus non solum directiones, tam secundum viam rationalem, quam iuxta Ptolemaei formam 4.

Which roughly translates to:

The tables of the first moveable, which are commonly called directions, which not only directions, both according to the rational way and according to the form of Ptolemy.

They had the great idea to make astrology charts take into account the ascension of each planet and use that as a division system within the chart.

People then continued to make his charts using that system.

Eventually pamphlets called 'tables of houses' were published using this system and since no other method was offered, they became more widely used.

These tables of houses list the degrees of latitude and the degree measurement of the houses, so someone wouldn't have to give themselves a headache calculating it using an Astrolabe or being friendly with someone trained in astronomy.

Brought to England

When the Placidus system was first 'brought' to England in 1711, it was violently opposed by some astrologers.

Richard Gibson, a Gosport-based 'Student of Astrology' wrote in 1711 in his book:

Flagellum Placidianum, or a whip for Placidianism wherein is detected and deservedly retorted the notorious absurdities and scandalous invectives made by Mr. Whalley (on his Translation of Ptolomy's Quadrapartite and his Treatise of Eclipses) against the laudable and genuine Astrology.

"Here is nothing but Egyptian Absoluteness and the power of monkish infallibility, zealously urged in Billingsgate rhetoric, all of which I could not read without just abhorrence and detestation." 5.

I can quite understand the frustrations! Mind you, I don't feel abhorrence or detestation with the Placidus system. I just like keeping things easy-to-understand for me, my clients, my students and my readers.

Astrologers already had a fab system that did everything they wanted it to. Then it got 'fashionable' to use a *totally* different system using **time** to divide the chart up.

Rather than mathematics or degrees.

Sidereal time to be precise.

Then there's a thing called 'diurnal semi-arcs' and it gets more and more complicated so there would be no way to calculate in your mind (which you can do with Equal House) how far away from the Ascendant a certain house would be.

Tables of Houses

The only way to use that system was/is to use what were/are called 'tables of houses'.

Here's what one looks like:

Early Astro Almanacs

These tables of houses got published in the U.K by a 26 year old Pisces entrepreneur called R.C Smith in his almanac (calendar of months and days with added astro/farming/weather info)

He hit on the idea of publishing the information that people needed to use to calculate charts and since he'd used the Placidus system, and it was complicated to do, his little magazine took off.

It was originally called *The Spirit of Partridge or the Astrologer's Pocket Companion* and later was titled *Raphael's Ephemeris*.

More information about the history of 'Raphael's Ephemeris' has been covered by Astrologer Kim Farnell http://www.kimfarnell.co.uk/raphael1.htm

No-one produced or *needed* to produce a table of house for the Equal House system as the chart was simply divided up in 30 degree segments.

Plus there wasn't any money to be made to do this and luckily for Smith, Raphael's Ephemeris sold very well.

Now computer programmes do all of this for us.

Computer Calculations

In the past, birth charts had to be made on paper, written out by hand. It could take quite a few hours to calculate everything correctly.

Before computers were invented, you'd have to locate the place the person was born, calculate how far away that was from Greenwich in London, convert local time to that time, add bits here and there. You'd have to take longitude and latitude into account.

Add in time differences like daylight saving, or War time or even double daylight saving.

If you're born on the West of a country your chart will be totally different to someone born on the East of a country.

It was SO complicated, I never would have been capable of doing it back then.

At some point in the 1980s all of these calculations which used to be made as on-paper measurements using those tables of houses and the ephemeris started to be calculated using computers, and the Placidus system simply carried over into online sites.

Astrology teachers taught the Placidus system and/or developed other systems such as Koch, Porphyry, Campanus and Regiomontanus.

Then in the year 2000 the ancient Whole sign system was researched, revitalised and written about by Robert Hand https://www.arhatmedia.com/whole_sign.html and that system was also adopted online.

Astrologer Chris Brennan has written more about it's history here https://hellenisticastrology.com/brennan-house-division.pdf

Today astro.com lists at least 12 house systems: https://www.astro.com/faq/fq_fh_owhouse_e.htm

Equal house still exists but as it can't be attributed to any one *person* in particular, and even though it's far easier to use, it was sadly dropped from favour.

Which I think is a dreadful shame!

Some schools still teach it, such as the Faculty for Astrological Studies.

Through the years astrology has taken twists and turns in various directions but one thing has remained constant.

Most people who 'discover' astrology for themselves want to know about their own chart and in doing so, they learn more about their own potential.

How fab is that!

Chapter Two

Why Using Equal House is Easy to Understand & Remember

The website that I use to teach my students is a Swiss one called Astrodienst.

The web address is https://www.astro.com/horoscope

The default system on there is Placidus so you will have to search around a bit to find a way to make your chart using the equal house system.

However, you won't have to suffer because I've made a video showing how to make it here:

https://youtu.be/NeRiGPkjpbk

I can also explain it in simple English here:

Calculating your Equal House Astro Chart the Easy Equal House Way

Go to https://www.astro.com/

Make an account with them.

It's free.

When you get to the first page go to:

FREE HOROSCOPES

Horoscope drawing and data

Extended chart selection

When you get to the **Extended Chart Selection** page you'll see the headings:

Birth data

Sections

Zodiac and houses

If you click the Zodiac and Houses box/section, the house system is set to the default (Placidus) system.

You can choose 'equal house' in the drop down box.

When you've inputted all your data, click "show chart" to view the chart you've created.

If you have done this correctly, you should see a chart with red and blue lines going through it, all the symbols for the signs of the Zodiac around the outside of the circle of the chart and the symbols for each planet somewhere inside the chart.

The chart should be divided into 12 equal segments and numbered from 1-12 in the inside.

These are house numbers and go anti-clockwise (counter-clockwise), around the circle.

In an Astrological chart, all the signs of the Zodiac progress around the chart in an anti-clockwise direction, in the same order that they are written in the ephemeris or on a website or magazine.

They start with Aries and progress to Pisces.

Katy's Chart

We are going to use the chart example of my sadly deceased youngest sister Katy.

She was born with Down's Syndrome. However our mother, even though she was a bit shocked when Katy was born, spent the rest of her life teaching and encouraging Katy, so she learnt to read and write. She had speech therapy. She had a few jobs. She even had a boyfriend. She was my 'best sister' and we had a wonderful bond.

(She also called herself 'best sister' to all our other siblings!)

Her early death in her 40s due to dementia hit me very hard.

Amazingly, my husband's older brother had Down's Syndrome too and he lived to be nearly 70 years old. A great age.

Katy was christened Katherine. I spelt her name Katy.

She later changed the spelling to Katie, so please excuse the different spellings I might use.

The Three Important Things

For astrology to work correctly you need to have three important pieces of information.

If you live in the USA, or France or some European countries and Scotland it will be easy to find as it will be on your birth certificate.

If you live in England or Wales it won't be quite so easy at all.

You will need your date, time and location of birth.

I was born in London in the afternoon.

Luckily my Auntie was heavily into Astrology and she wrote my birth time down in her Ephemeris.

Thank you Auntie Jo!

Date, Location, Time

The *date* will let us know what sign of the Zodiac you are.

The *location* will take into account the 'view' of the sky.

And the *time* will determine what sign of the Zodiac your chart starts in and your Ascendant sign.

Here is what Katy's Astro chart looks like.

Name: ♀ Katie English
born on Tu., 17 January 1967
in London, ENG (UK)
0w10, 51n30
Natal Chart (Method: Web Style / equal)
Sun sign: Capricorn
Ascendant: Aries

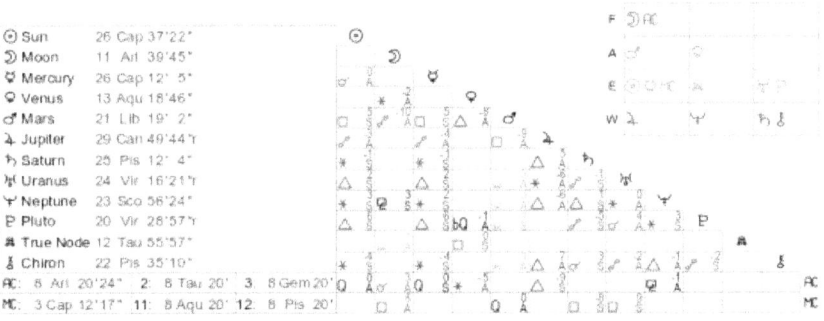

31

Let me explain a bit about what you'll 'see' when you create a chart for the first time.

If you're using the default image settings on astro.com you'll see a circle with the symbols for the signs of the Zodiac written around the outside rim of the circle.

A set of horns shaped like a V for Aries, two squiggly lines for the sign of Aquarius and an arrow for the sign of Sagittarius etc

Memorise those symbols, they'll turn up a lot in Astrology and save us writing the word for each sign.

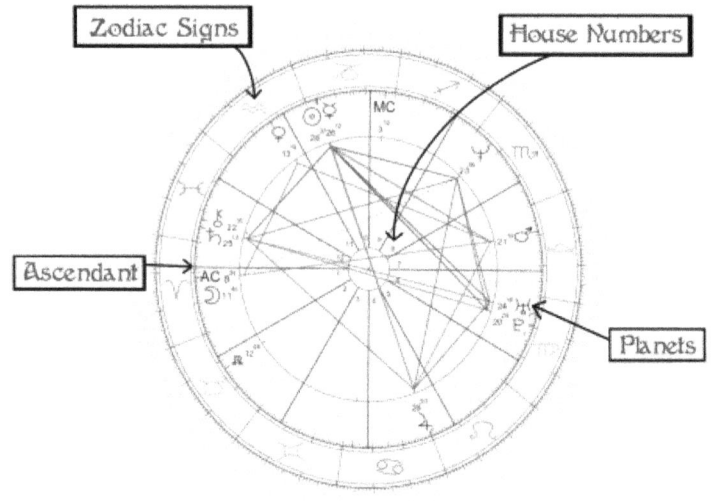

Chart showing main themes

The Ascendant

At the quarter to nine/8.45am position are the initials AC, more about that in next chapter.

Numbers 1-12

If you look closely in the centre of the circle will be the numbers 1-12, these are the houses. They're written anti-clockwise around the circle.

Then there are the symbols for each planet.

There's a cheat-sheet at the bottom left of the chart with the symbol and then it's name written next to it.

In Katy's chart it says Sun 26 Capricorn 37' (minutes) 22" (seconds)

Moon 11 Aries 38' 45"

Aspect Lines

There will also be lots of coloured lines going from planet to planet.

Red lines, blue lines, sometimes black dotted lines and/or green lines

These are mathematical degrees that each planet is away from each other.

Don't worry about those at the moment.

They're called Aspects.

More Than One Sign in a House

Depending on what time of day you were born, some of your houses may have more than one sign in them. Unless you were born at exactly 0 degrees of an Ascendant sign, ALL your houses will contain more than one sign.

In Katy's case, there are two signs within *each* house.

For instance:

In house number 4, she has the signs Cancer and Leo

Her Jupiter (looks like the number 4) is in the sign of Cancer 29 degrees, 49 44 and has a little r next to it.

Any planet you have that was retrograde when you were born will have that little r next to it.

The graph bottom right of the chart with all those little boxes explains a bit more about the Aspects that are in her chart.

Aspect Graph

If you look at the vertical Sun line you'll see she has the Sun opposition Jupiter.

You read this by looking down the Sun line, then horizontally across to the symbol for Jupiter and directly in/under the Sun line there is another symbol that looks like a dumbbell.

It's written in red.

This means she has Sun opposition Jupiter.

In the line above is a square.

If you look across to the right you'll see the symbol for Mars, so this means she has 'Sun Square Mars'.

Aspects in her Chart

You'll see both of these Aspects in the chart itself. Find the Sun in the 10th house.

There's a red line going down the chart from there to her Jupiter in the 4th house.

Sun opposition Jupiter.

Qualities Box

The last box I'll explain is to the bottom right of the chart.

It has the initials F, A, E, W down the side

And C, F, M going across

This lets us know how many Fire, Air, Earth and Water planets or parts she has

And Cardinal, Fixed and Mutable planets.

In Katy's case she has a total of seven Cardinal points: Moon, AC, Mars, Sun, Mercury, MC and Jupiter

They're divided again into Fire, Air, Earth, Water.

Have a look at your chart and see what you've got.

Now you're doing Astrology !

Well done!

One of the nicest things about the Equal House system is it's much easier to use.

Whatever is the degree number of the Ascendant, will also be the degree number of the *beginning* of every other house.

Let me explain.

The Degree of the Ascendant

Each sign of the Zodiac is 30 degrees. All the 12 signs together equal 360 degrees which is the circumference of a circle. And a circle is the shape that we use to represent the placement of the planets on the day you were born.

Katy has an Aries Ascendant of 8 degrees, 20 minutes and 24 seconds

It's shown at the quarter to nine/8.45am position on the chart, next to the initials AC.

It reads 8 20

You can find the exact degrees on the box bottom left of the chart

It reads AC: 8 Aries 20'24"

In the chart, the computer programme has rounded down the degrees to just minutes, not seconds because there isn't room in the chart itself to include the seconds as well.

So her first house starts in the sign of Aries at 8 degrees 20 minutes.

This made her quite forceful and confident.

She certainly could speak up for herself if she wasn't happy about something!

Her Moon is also in Aries, and is very near to the Ascendant.

On the chart its listed as 11 40

But if you check the box at the bottom it's been rounded up so that reads 11 Aries 39' 45"

Which translates to 11 degrees Aries, 39 minutes and 45 seconds.

Now, because her Ascendant is 8 degrees, every other house in her chart will start at 8 degrees.

So her second house starts 8 degrees Taurus, her third house starts 8 degrees Gemini and so on, all the way round the circle until we get back to the Ascendant.

Every house is 30 degrees big, but starts at 8 degrees.

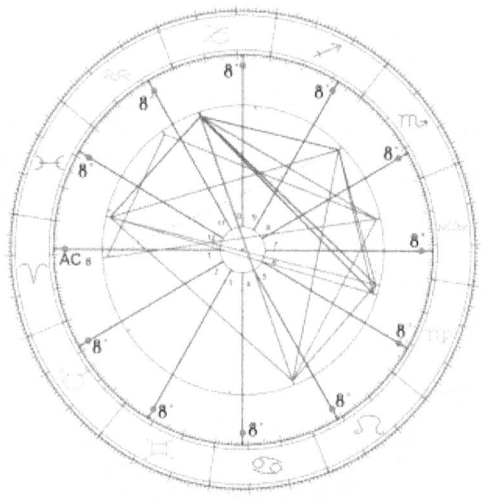

Showing the 8 degrees start of each house in Katy's chart

So if you wanted to calculate in your mind what sign her 9th house would be

Nine signs on from Aries is Sagittarius.

Easy!!

It also means that if someone says to you they know their Ascendant sign, you won't need to use any calculations to work out what sign will be on the beginning of any other house in the chart.

Just count on from the sign of the Ascendant to the house number you want to understand.

The 7th house will be in the opposite sign of the Ascendant and you'll know how they tackle relationships.

One of the most confusing things about learning Astrology is all the possible combinations you could have for what's in each house and how that planet operates.

The Longing for Everything

Students of Astrology long for a computer programme that will give every combination of every planet, in every sign in each of the 12 houses.

I'm sure someone somewhere has made that programme by now.

However since there are 10 planets that we use and 12 houses and also 12 signs, the maths adds up to a possible 1,440 different combinations. And if someone was writing that computer programme, they'd have to make 1,440 entries explaining those combinations. Most computer programmes give you planet-in-sign and planet-in-house. As yet, I haven't seen planet-in-sign-in-house. But maybe one day that will happen.

It also doesn't take into account having more than one planet in a house or even none.

How do we make sense of this?

This is where keywords really help and I've developed a few that might help you.

Sign Keywords

Some are from the titles of my series of Sun sign books. I used rather cheeky titles.

I've changed the keywords for the Virgo, Capricorn and Pisces books as they were titled: *How to Soothe a Virgo, How to Cheer Up a Capricorn* and *How to Survive a Pisces*.

Keywords for the signs

Aries = Appreciate

Taurus = Satisfy

Gemini = Listen

Cancer = Care

Leo = Lavish

Virgo = Perfect

Libra = Love

Scorpio = Trust

Sagittarius = Believe in

Capricorn = Be Serious

Aquarius = Be Friends

Pisces = Be Intuitive

Planet Keywords

Each planet has far more than one word to describe its meaning or how it operates. For the purposes of making what I'm telling you easier, I've narrowed them down to no more than three.

There are books you can buy telling you more information about each planet, where/when it was discovered and how Astrologers have utilised that planet for interpretation purposes.

All of my books do that.

Keywords for Planets

Sun = ego or self

Moon = emotions

Mercury = communication

Mars = action, aggression or energy

Venus = love, taste and/or money

Jupiter = luck, higher learning

Saturn = responsibility

Uranus = sudden happenings

Neptune = intuition

Pluto = deep change and transformation

We will come back to these keywords as we progress with your learning.

To help you remember everything, you could print off your chart and write the words next to the signs and the planets in your own chart.

Chapter Three

House Meanings & Keywords

There is a similarity between the houses meanings and the signs of the Zodiac.

House one is like the sign Aries, representing the self.

The difference is subtle.

The differences are things like the eight house meaning investments, that's not strictly Scorpio territory, so try not to confuse the two things.

Stick with the keywords and it will help you stay clear.

The house meanings haven't changed too much over the years but if you were to read very old astrology books you'll likely see some rather scary terms.

Here's an example of Mars in the eight house:

Legacies; if with bad aspects, possibilities of disputes re legacies or inheritance, or of violent manner of death; bereavements.

Remember what Astrology was used for many years ago.

It was used to make sense of wars, to defeat enemies, to illustrate ambition, and to deal with inheritance and lots of money matters. They were also a lot more obsessed with death.

Today Astrology is mostly used to understand 'the self' and it has wonderfully adapted to do that.

Obviously people still want to know if they'll marry, get a job, have a baby, change career, recover from an illness or move house.

These are human concerns.

I don't think they change much.

The joy of astrology is learning about your place in the world.

Are you following the path that suits your sign and/or your planet placements?

For instance, having the Sun in the 5th house is completely different to having it in the 10th house.

The fifth house is all about creativity and the Sun is 'happy' in this house. The tenth house is all about ambition, so it will change how the Sun expresses itself.

So here are the keywords for each house.

House Keywords

Keywords for Houses

1st house = the self

2nd house = finances

3rd house = communication

4th house = the home/roots

5th house = creativity

6th house = health & routine/work

7th house = the other, (opposite of the first house) close personal relationship/s

8th house = sex/birth/death/investments

9th house = philosophy, further education, travel

10th house = career

11th house = friendships/groups

12th house = the hidden self

Now, let's make life easier by using just these words to describe the combinations you have in your chart.

You have Sun in Capricorn in the 5th house:

You take your creativity seriously

You can now make a sentence for each combo you have.

Try again…

Uranus in Scorpio in the 3rd house

Trust the suddenness of communication

Maybe move words into a different order for your combos until they feel right ...for you.

Again, print off your chart and add the meanings into each of your houses and study them.

Do they feel right for you?

Chapter Four

Chart Examples

Let's use a nice easy chart, one of a person you might have heard of and has an accurate time, date and location of birth.

Queen Elizabeth the second of Great Britain.

She had a Capricorn Ascendant.

Sun in Taurus in the 4th house

Moon in Leo in the 7th house

Using the keywords we learned earlier we could say:

A Serious lady (Capricorn Asc) who needs to feel satisfied (Sun in Taurus) in her home (4th house) and who emotionally likes to lavish attention (Moon in Leo) on her partner (7th house), or be lavished with his attention.

That little sentence accurately describes Queen Elizabeth.

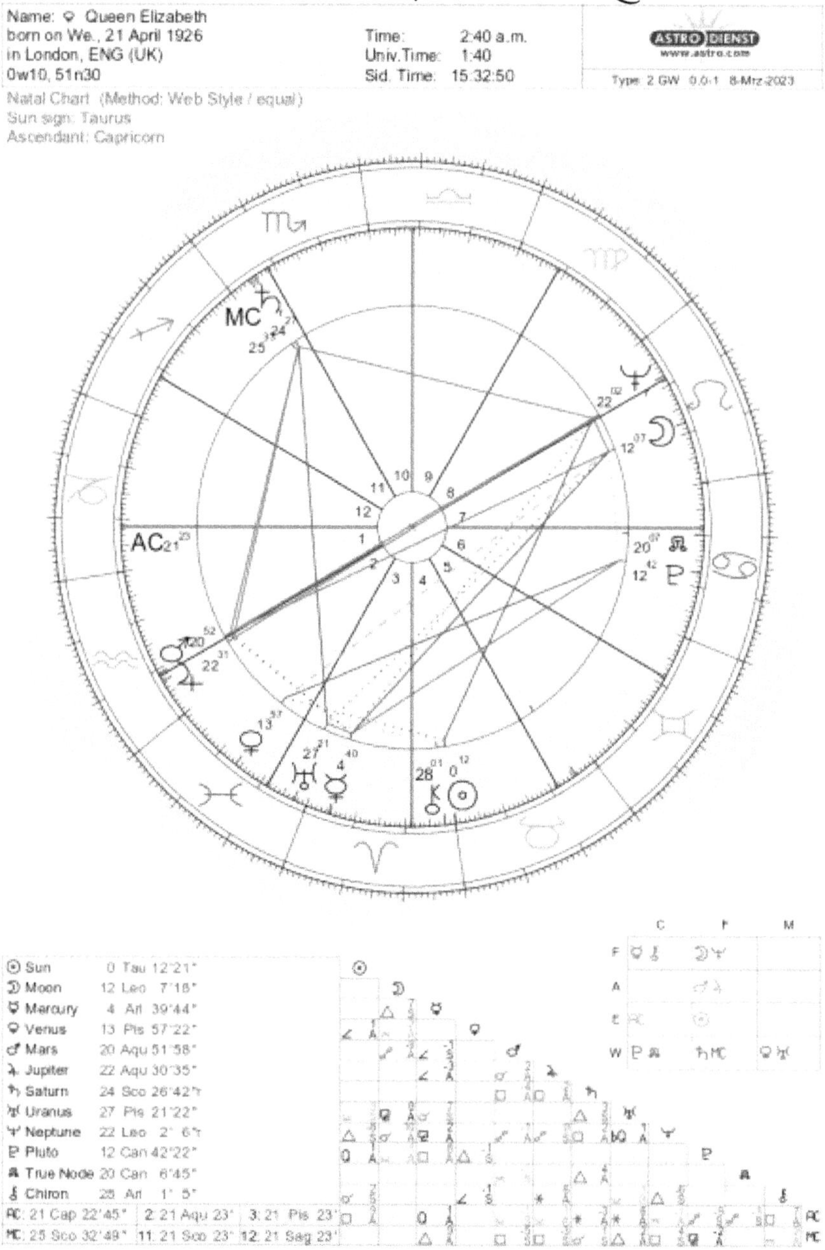

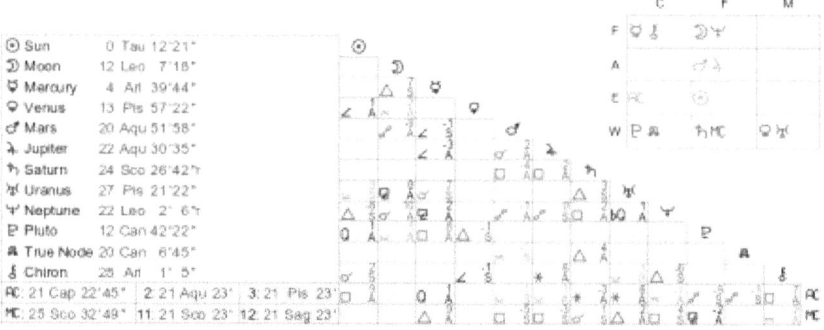

Let's work with another chart.

Let's use a student who studied with me.

Astrology Student

She has a Virgo Ascendant,

Sun in Pisces in the 6th house

Moon in Cancer in the 10th house

This is a lady who is aiming for perfection (Virgo Asc) and who needs to feel intuitive (Sun in Pisces) and who emotionally needs to care (Moon Cancer) about her career (Moon in 10th), or be in work where her emotions are helpful.

Name: ♀ (5.3.1971)
born on Fr., 5 March 1971
in Dorking, ENG (UK)
0w20, 51n14

Time: 7:10 p.m.
Univ. Time: 18:10
Sid. Time: 5:00:01

Natal Chart (Method: Web Style / equal)
Sun sign: Pisces
Ascendant: Virgo

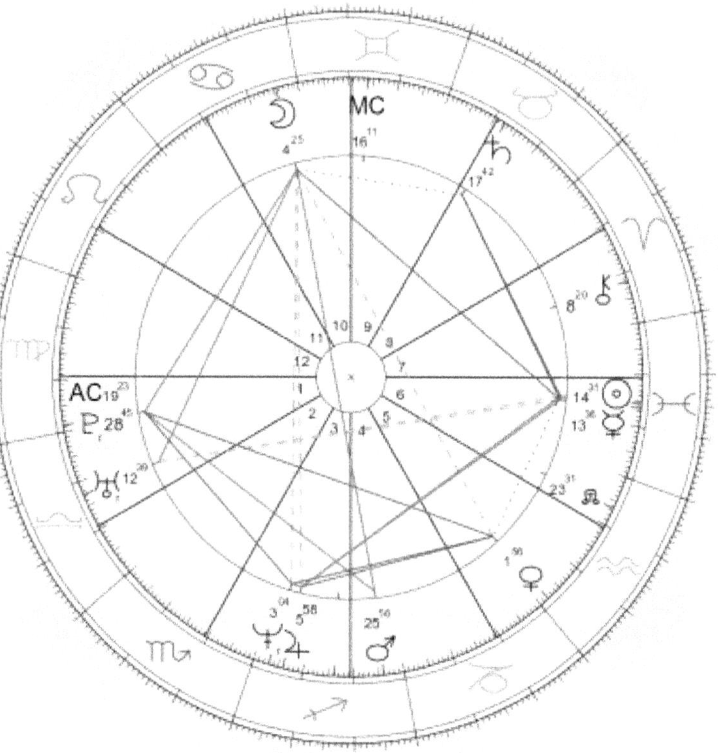

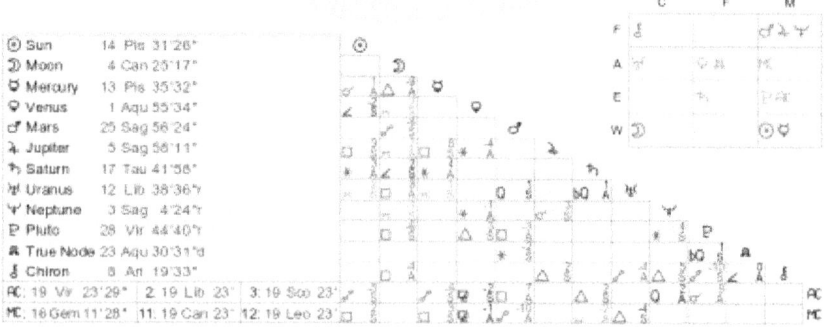

☉ Sun	14 Pis 31'26"
☽ Moon	4 Can 25'17"
☿ Mercury	13 Pis 35'32"
♀ Venus	1 Aqu 55'34"
♂ Mars	25 Sag 56'24"
♃ Jupiter	5 Sag 58'11"
♄ Saturn	17 Tau 41'58"
♅ Uranus	12 Lib 38'36"r
♆ Neptune	3 Sag 4'24"
♇ Pluto	28 Vir 44'40"r
☊ True Node	23 Aqu 30'31"d
⚷ Chiron	8 Ari 19'33"

AC: 19 Vir 23'29" | 2: 19 Lib 23' | 3: 19 Sco 23'
MC: 19 Gem 11'28" | 11: 19 Can 23' | 12: 19 Leo 23'

54

Obviously there are other words to describe each sign, each house and each planet.

This is just to give you a starting point with understanding an Astro chart.

All too often when beginning to learn Astrology there can be soooooo much to think about your brain can become somewhat frazzled.

Don't worry though.

After a time spent practicing with lots of different charts, you'll begin to understand that there are differences between us humans. And it's those differences that help us make sense of our place in this world. It will also help us understand others.

Making Unhelpful Judgements

Now you can also end up, if you're not careful, making serious judgements about a chart and telling yourself that *'all Scorpios are jealous'* or *'every Gemini is chatty'* especially if you read older Astrology books.

Be careful of those sorts of judgements as they are not true.

I know a number of very quiet, rather shy Geminis and equally some Scorpios who are very chatty!

Everyone has ev*ery* sign in their chart.

They might not have a planet in every sign, or even a planet in many houses but we all have every sign from Aries to Pisces in our charts.

Obviously some people use their born talents in better ways than others, so it's our job as Astrologers to guide our clients to do the best for themselves using the potential in their chart.

Or we can learn ourselves how to make the best of the life we have, that's represented in our own natal chart.

Let's do another chart

Let's go back to my little sister's chart.

Katy English

Aries Ascendant

Sun in Capricorn in the 10th

Moon in Aries in the first

Whenever we have a planet in the first house, especially the Moon, then the emotions are going to be very near the surface.

Keywords:

1st house: self

Aries : appreciate

Moon : emotions

Katy wants to have her own (1st house) emotions (Moon) appreciated (in Aries)

Sun in Capricorn in the 10th :

Katy takes herself seriously (Capricorn Sun) when it comes to her career (10th house)

Let's do Mars in Libra in the 7th house

Mars : action/aggression/energy

Libra: Love

7th house : close personal relationships

Katy loves to be a bit aggressive (Mars) or energetic with her partner/s (7th house)

Don't make things complicated. Stick with these keywords until you feel more confident.

Mars is important in Katy's chart as her Ascendant is Aries and the ruling planet to Aries = Mars

See chapter Six for more info on this.

Let's do another combination.

Loving to Have Friends

Venus (the goddess of love), in Aquarius (the sign of friendship), in the 11th house (of friendships).

She loved to have friends.

Now I know most people like to have friends, but what we are describing here is that having friends was *super* important for her.

In reality, whenever she met someone, she would ask for their date of birth and their address.

She would then write their name and birthday in her calendar, then every week would send birthday cards that she had made to each person who had a birthday that week.

Some weeks she would send more than 10 cards to various people. She kept this up for most of her life until she got dementia in her late 40s.

I still have her address book and calendar.

Over the years her calendar got pretty packed. She also religiously recorded their home addresses.

I was truly amazed at her ability to do this as not only did she have Downs Syndrome but she also had chronic psoriasis and it made her feel uncomfortable sometimes.

However, it didn't stop her from spending time every week hand-making birthday cards and posting them to the people she'd met and all family members.

When she was younger she'd write to and send cards to famous people or characters from soap operas. As she got older, she included in her list, people that she met at her volunteer work or who helped her in any way.

She'd always remember what pets people owned and would mention them in her letters or cards.

Her social life brought her contentment and the placement of Venus in Aquarius, which is anyway the sign of friendship, in the 11th house, was perfectly represented in her chart.

If this wasn't a true expression of Venus-in-Aquarius-in-the-11th-house, I don't know what is!

Chapter Five

Empty Houses and Sign & House Rulers Level Two: Intermediate

Empty Houses

One thing you'll come across when you first start learning Astrology is finding out that there are gaps in your chart.

Arrrgh Mary!

I've got an empty house!

What does that mean?

Don't panic.

Everyone will have at least two empty houses, purely due to the fact that we're only using ten planets and there are twelve houses.

And some people can have 8 empty houses, especially if they were born during an outer-planetary conjunction. See my book The Astrology of Indigos.

Now we have to go a little deeper into Astrological theory.

Sign Rulers

Each sign of the Zodiac has a planet that 'looks after' it.

We call them Rulers.

Like some King Or Queen ruling a country.

Don't forget Astrology is an ancient craft and quite a lot of the terminology has barely altered over the centuries.

So here are the accepted rulers to each sign:

Leo's ruler is The Sun

Cancer's ruler is The Moon

Gemini and Virgo's ruler is Mercury

Taurus and Libra's ruler is Venus

Aries' ruler is Mars

Sagittarius' ruler is Jupiter

Capricorn's ruler is Saturn

Aquarius' ruler is Uranus

Pisces' ruler is Neptune

Scorpio's ruler is Pluto

In more ancient Astrology, before the three outer planets were discovered Mars ruled Aries and Scorpio, Saturn ruled Aquarius and Capricorn and Jupiter ruled Sagittarius and Pisces.

To make it even easier, think of sign rulers as planets certain signs have an affinity for.

Or that planets operate in a more 'normal' manner when they are in certain signs.

Now

Back to houses.

Let's use a chart example to make this a tad easier.

In Queen Elizabeth's chart she has four empty houses : 5, 9, 10 and 12

Now you could be thinking that because her 5th house of creativity and children is empty, she therefore she wouldn't have any kiddies.

She actually had four children.

She gave birth to Charles, Anne, Andrew and Edward.

So let's use the ruler to her 5th house.

Her 5th house starts in the sign of Taurus (which is a fertile sign).

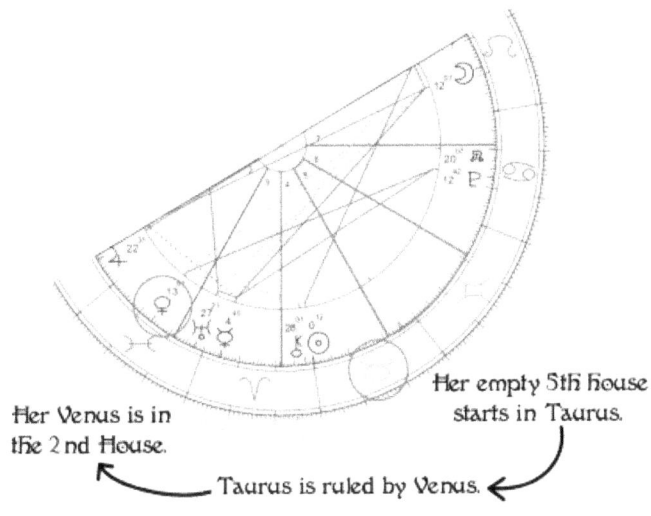

Queen Elizabeth's Empty 5th house and Taurus Ruler = Venus

Taurus is ruled by Venus (another fertile planet) and her Venus is located in the 2nd house of money.

Maybe she viewed her children as a financial 'investment'. She certainly had to have children otherwise there would be no-one to inherit the title or carry on the Royal line.

Which if you ask me must be a big concern to a royal family. If they don't have any kids, the family ceases to exist.

Her 9th house is also empty.

It starts in the sign of Virgo, which is ruled by Mercury and her natal Mercury is located in her 3rd house of siblings and short journeys.

So a connection between these two houses means she certainly liked travelling. Maybe she enjoyed writing or talking about her travels?

Natural House Rulers

Now, because Astrologers like to complicate things we can also have a thing called House Rulers.

If we were to imagine the circle of an astrological chart and that each sign of the Zodiac was in the 'natural' order that they are in the Astrological calendar:

Aries, Taurus, Gemini, Cancer, Leo, Virgo, Libra, Scorpio, Sagittarius, Capricorn, Aquarius and Pisces.

We already know what the Rulers are to each of those signs.

Now we imagine (and there's a lot of imagining in Astrology) that whatever order the signs are in a chart, we'll ignore that and just imagine that the houses 'normal' order is as above.

So the 'Ruler' to the first house (first sign of Aries) is Mars

The Ruler to the second house (second sign of Taurus) is Venus

And so on…

Remember of course that none of this is literal.

Houses don't exist in 'real life'.

And Rulers are a construct that Astrologers have developed over time.

It didn't happen overnight!

Now I have to say this took me a little time to get my head around, so don't be dismayed or worried if you can't grasp it first time.

I've got Mercury in Pisces retrograde so my Mercury not only isn't happy in the sign of Pisces, it also easily gets confused and works best by imitation, rote learning and repeating things over and over ...

Going back to house Rulers

If you have a planet in the house which in the natural order has a ruler, then that planet is 'happy' in that house.

It might not be happy in that *sign,* but it could cheer up a little being in that *house.*

So let's go back to The Queen's chart and see if she has any planets in their 'natural' homes.

And yes, she does.

She has three planets 'happy' in certain houses.

Keep in mind the order of the Zodiac and each sign's ruler. Here they are in order.

The Natural Rulers to the Houses.

Astrologers also consider the 'natural' house rulers.

If we remember that the signs of the Zodiac go from Aries to Pisces, each standard house/sign has a Ruler.

They go in this order:

First house: Aries - Mars

Second house : Taurus - Venus

Third house : Gemini - Mercury

Fourth house : Cancer - The Moon

Fifth house: Leo - The Sun

Sixth house : Virgo - Mercury

Seventh house : Libra - Venus

Eighth house : Scorpio - Pluto (or old ruler Mars)

Ninth house : Sagittarius - Jupiter

Tenth house : Capricorn - Saturn

Eleventh house : Aquarius - Uranus (old ruler Saturn)

Twelfth house : Pisces - Neptune (old ruler Jupiter)

The Queen has Mars in the first house

Venus in the 2nd house

Mercury in the 3rd house

So those planets are happier in those houses and won't do daft stuff and are more likely to operate to her benefit.

Don't get confused, house rulers are different to sign rulers.

Interpreting Empty Houses

You can watch a webinar I made of this on my YouTube channel here: https://youtu.be/JVCyBaHCT7A

It will certainly be the case that you will have certain houses that are empty of any planets because there are 12 houses and only 10 planets that we use.

Working in exactly the same way as we have already, work out the ruler to the house you don't have a planet in.

My second house of money is completely empty of planets.

It starts in the sign of Virgo.

The ruler to Virgo is Mercury and my Mercury is located in the 7th house.

So you could say:

"I can make money from communication/writing (Mercury) about health (Virgo) and relationships (7th house)"

Which I have done as I wrote a book about Homeopathy and an Astrology book about lovers.

An empty house will happen, it just means that the house that's empty has no *activity* in it.

It's not a good or a bad thing.

Houses that do have planets are more active and where there's activity there might be more interest or more focus.

The house ruler to my second house, which starts in the sign of Libra, is Venus and my Venus is in the 6th house of work

So maybe *I enjoy working*?

Which again I do.

So we can have two rulers to each house

The normal Aries-Pisces *sign* rulers and also the individual to your chart's *house* rulers.

I prefer the individual ruler but there are arguments for considering both.

Maybe you have Venus in Aquarius in your 7th house

The ruler to the house is Uranus, because it starts in the sign of Aquarius

The ruler to the 'natural' 7th house is Venus because Libra is the 7th sign of the Zodiac

So your *planet* is 'happy' there as it's in its 'natural house'.

Your *sign* ruler will be in another house.

Now, you could of course have a Taurus Asc and a Scorpio descendant/7th house and have Pluto there in its natural *sign* but not the house ruler.

Pluto isn't especially happy in the 7th as he prefers to be in the 8th, it's house ruler.

Really Bad Things....Not

One thing I've learned from years of teaching astrology is that it's very easy to get totally worked-up about a planet in a sign in a house conjunct some other planet and your mind goes all over the place imagining that it's a really, really bad thing and you're going to die any minute and your whole life will be a mess.

Astrology doesn't work like that.

It's a system to help you understand yourself and/or others and if you immediately only think about all the negatives of your planetary placements, it's not going to be helpful is it?

Make astrology helpful.

Don't make it a cross for you to bear.

Don't use it as an excuse or a 'reason' even.

Astrology just 'is'.

And it will show you, if you look carefully, how wonderful you actually are!

Chapter Six

Chart Rulers
Level Three: Advanced

OK. You've done really well to get to this chapter. Maybe take a rest if you've got this far and understood everything I've told you. Maybe make lots of charts including your own and those you know well.

The only way to learn Astrology properly is to make lots (and I mean LOTS) of charts.

That way you're familiar with the differences between them, the things that are the same, the things that stand out. And you'll eventually start to notice things you didn't 'see' before because you were so busy being overwhelmed by everything.

One thing I have noticed with 'newbies' or beginner Astrologers is that they become very easily overwhelmed by all the things that are in a chart and what-they-might-mean and they get cross with themselves that they don't 'know' it all.

Trust me, no Astrologer knows everything!

And we're not aiming at knowing and understand *everything*!

In this book we are just learning a little more about Astrology and are tackling the most difficult part of it all, with the houses.

It's much easier to learn about the types of planets and even the signs that they are in.

What is far more difficult is learning off-by-heart all the possible permutations that can occur.

You can make it easier for yourself by using a good computer programme.

I started with a very basic programme that was actually written by someone who I later found out wasn't even an Astrologer!

What he was though, was a very good writer and he was obviously using some sort of reference work to make the interpretations that he did.

It became more obvious when I used the programme when he said things like:

> *"The Ninth House, House of Philosophy & Travel*
>
> *If an astrologer ever comes out with the charming old cliche that they can "see foreign travel" in your chart, it is pretty much a certainty that they have seen something connected to Sagittarius in your chart.... "*

Which made it pretty clear that *he wasn't* an Astrologer !!

Make sure you use one that is written without scaring yourself or making it seem as if there is only ONE interpretation for any given placement.

The is no ONE way to do, or learn anything.

I'm just giving you what I've found worked for me when I started and what now helps learners who work with me.

So.

We've covered all the houses, all the signs, planet and house rulers

And there's one rulership left.

Chart Rulers.

This is where we determine which planet is THE most important one in your chart.

This is the one that holds the prize for being the one that will determine your outlook on life and how challenging or easy your life might be.

I like chart rulers A LOT and use them everyday when I work with clients and analyse their charts.

There are two ways to use them.

You can use them to find out what's important for the person.

You can also use them when you're considering transits.

I won't go into transits here but just to say a transiting planet is one that's moving through the sky right now and will or won't make an impact in your natal chart.

I describe them as 'passing traffic'.

Chart Rulers

Whatever *sign* your Ascendant is in, that sign (as we have already learned) has a Ruling planet

My chart starts in the sign of Leo (I'm not shy!) so my chart ruler is The Sun.

My Sun-in-Pisces is located in my 7th house of relationships, so being married is very important to me.

Leo and The Sun are positive signs and people with a Leo Ascendant (almost) always want to know about the positive side of life.

I once was criticised by my son for *being* positive: *"Oh, you're always so positive about things Mum"* he said.

As if being positive was something bad ! Ho ho, coming from someone with Mercury in Scorpio and has a Capricorn Moon.

I just laughed inwardly.

I *like* being positive! And what you like doing or being goes with more flow...

I also track the sign/house the transiting Sun is moving through to know where to put my energy that month.

House Location of Chart Ruler

When you've worked out your chart ruler planet, pay attention to where that planet is located in your chart.

What house is it in?

Is it 'happy' in that house?

If you have an Aries Ascendant and Mars is in your first house, then that planet will be 'happier' in that house.

You can also track the transits for that planet and wherever its transiting and whatever sign it might be in today, could be something you keep an eye on.

I won't go into transits, that's for another book.

All we are covering in this book is natal astrology.

The stuff you were born with, not what's happening today or might happen tomorrow.

Or even what happened yesterday.

Natal Astrology is learning about your own chart and what *potential* lies there.

Are you living to your full potential?

Go back to the keywords to get more info about chart rulers.

Brief Meanings of House Location of Chart Rulers

Ruler of the first in the first: you need to consider your 'self' first before others. Look after number one.

Ruler of the first in the second: money will play an important part of your life. Having it or not having it.

Ruler of the first in the third: communication of ideas will be very important for you.

Ruler of the first in the fourth: your home and family will be the main focus of your life.

Ruler of the first in the fifth: creativity, romance, babies, anything creative will be where you're happiest.

Ruler of the first in the sixth: your concerns will be your work and your own health, or those of others.

Ruler of the first in the seventh : you will feel more complete when you're in a close personal relationship.

Ruler of the first in the eight : Sex, money, investments and/or the occult could feature highly in your life.

Ruler of the first in the ninth: you'll enjoy long-distance travel and/or higher learning and you will need to feel as if you're in touch with your higher purpose.

Ruler of the first in the tenth: your career will be of utmost importance to you. For good or bad.

Ruler of the first in the eleventh: your friendship circle or tribe will be where your energies might need to be.

Ruler of the first in the twelfth: you could be shy, you need to be in the background in some way and prefer your own company and maybe silence.

Outer Planet Rulers

There are three outer planets : Uranus, Neptune and Pluto.

If you have an Aquarius, Pisces or Scorpio Ascendant, your chart rulers are going to be Uranus, Neptune or Pluto in that order.

Uranus has an 84 year cycle.

Neptune and Pluto take over a hundred years to circuit the Sun.

Neptune can spend approx 13 years in each sign.

And Pluto can spend approximately 15 years in each sign of the Zodiac. Sometimes it spends more than that, depending on what sign it's going through as its orbit is elongated.

What we need to keep in mind is what ruler it is and how it affects your chart and your outlook on life.

If you have an Aquarius Ascendant, Uranus is your Ruler and you need to make sure you've always got an 'exit' plan lined-up. As Uranus is such a freedom loving planet, you're going to want freedom of thought and speech and anything you perceive that gets in your way of that, you're more likely to butt against it.

If you have a Pisces Ascendant, Neptune will be your chart ruler.

Where is it located in your chart?

What sign is it in?

In what house area of life do you need to go-with-the-flow and use your intuition?

If you have a Scorpio Ascendant, Pluto is your chart Ruler.

You won't want to deal with trivialities and function best when you can go deeply into something.

Look and see where your natal Pluto is located.

Is this where you transform things?

Is this where you can feel 'power', 'empowerment' or 'disempowerment'.

The house your natal Pluto is in will be where you focus like a laser-beam.

And you can consider the oldies chart rulers if you want.

Mars is the other ruler to Scorpio

Chart rulers are e*xtremely* important and can only be determined if you have an accurate time of birth.

If you don't have the time, think about planet rulers and the signs your planets are in.

There are ways to give yourself a headache using declinations/debilities and dignities but I would recommend to only get into those when you've grasped all these basics that I'm writing about.

I personally think chart rulers are sometimes more important than any other ruler.

It gives you an idea of what's important for the person..

So let me break down the rulers again and why I think the rulers are so important.

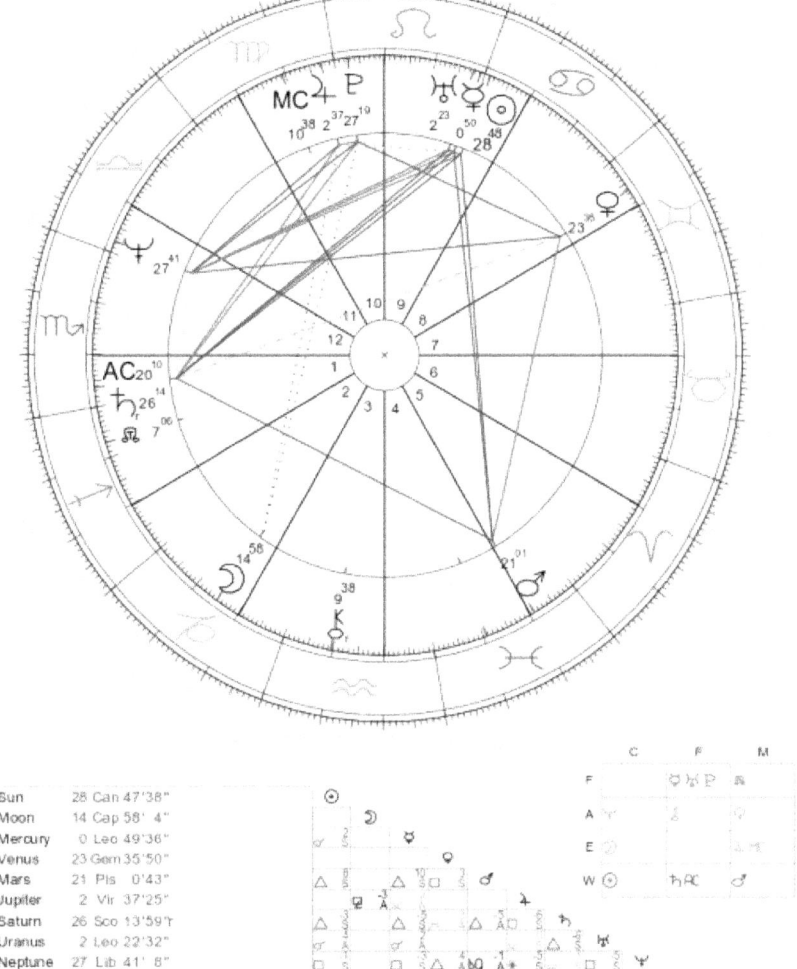

83

Podcast Person Example Chart

Let's use another example: Podcast person (PP)

Scorpio Ascendant.

Sun Cancer in the 9th house

Moon Capricorn in the 2nd House

Saturn is only a few degrees away from the Ascendant, so it's an important planet in their chart.

Any planet less than 8 degrees away from the Asc, either way, so less than 8 degrees, which will place it in the 12th house or more than 8 degrees, which will place it in the 1st house can be considered 'conjunct' the Ascendant.

But for the purposes of this chapter, we'll just consider the chart ruler.

Scorpio is ruled by 'modern' Pluto and oldie Mars

Natal Pluto is in the 10th house in the sign of Leo 27 degrees

Natal Mars is located in the 5th house in the sign of Pisces.

So this person could get very, very worried about their career.

They might even feel paranoid or passionate (there's no in between with Pluto!) and could worry about work colleagues ganging-up on them or working against them until they feel they can trust them.

On the positive side they might put ALL their energies into their job and live and breathe it.

Mars in the 5th again there could be 'wars' about children/romance/risks.

Now, on the point of 'where-are-their-planets' their Mars is *just* into the 5th house.

Remembering what I've told you before, keep in mind the exact degree of the Asc, because every following house will be the same degree.

Podcast Person (PP) has a Scorpio Asc, 20 degrees, 9 mins, 42 seconds which the software rounds-up to ASC 20, 10 on the picture.

If you look closely at the listed planets in the box bottom left with all the symbols for the planets written in black and the degrees are written in blue, you'll see the correct exact info.

Always check these boxes at the bottom before you make a judgment about things.

Now PP has their Mars Pisces 21 degrees, 0 mins, 43 seconds

We already know that their Asc is 20 degree, so if a planet is 21 degrees it'll be at the beginning of the house.

Astrology Student Chart

Astrology Student has a Virgo Ascendant, so the ruler to her chart is Mercury.

Her Mercury is in the sign of Pisces in the 6th house of health.

This makes her 6th house extra important.

Mercury is the planet about communication and also what we like to talk about.

So she likes to 'talk about her/others health' and is very clued-up on health issues.

Queen Elizabeth's Chart

Her chart starts in the sign Capricorn with a Capricorn Ascendant, so her chart Ruler is Saturn

So if I had done a reading for her (as if!) I'd say: *"Keep an eye on Saturn as it's an important planet for you."*

Her natal Saturn was in the sign of Scorpio retrograde in the 11th house of friends. I don't know about you, but I never read anything about the Queen having *lots* of friends. I would expect that the ones she had, she'd have to trust them a lot.

Katy's Chart

In Katy's chart as it starts in the sign of Aries, her chart ruler is Mars, because Mars rules Aries.

And her natal Mars is located in the 7th house of relationships.

So having a relationship was important for her.

And she got energy from knowing her boyfriend.

They would speak on the phone every week and that phone-call was super important for her.

Interestingly her boyfriend was an Aries and the ruling planet to Aries is Mars, so it's as if she manifested a relationships that suited her chart. She wanted someone dynamic, and he was certainly that. When he was little he used to literally run away, on his own and try to get to the train station to watch the trains.

He was fearless!

And that was something Katy enjoyed.

Chapter Seven

Exercises

In this part of the book we are actually going to work with your own chart, if you haven't done this already.

Now I know full well that you're not here with me, but I'll pretend you are to make it easier for you.

We're going to work through your own chart and get some answers for you.

Make an account and your chart on Astro.com as instructed in Chapter One.

Print off Your Astro Chart

If you print off your chart it will make it much easier to work with.

You can also write things on it, until you can remember signs and/or planet symbols.

The major disadvantage of looking at it on a screen is you'll either be distracted by other things or even worse you'll miss the teeny bits of writing that are harder to see on screens.

We're now going to work with what you're actually looking at.

I can't stress more strongly why it's important to use Astro.com as many websites use different ways to 'view' a chart and if you use another website or app you won't be seeing what I'm now going to share with you.

And since I'm not actually in the room with you, I won't be able to identify what you're looking at.

And trust me!

There's LOTS to see in an Astro.com chart!

Use the default 'look' of your chart and you should have a blue circle on the outside of your chart and red/blue/black and possibly green lines going from planet to planet.

They're called Aspects and we're not covering them in this book.

Bottom Left Box

Bottom left of your chart will have all your planets written in a box starting with the Sun at the top and (possibly) Chiron at the bottom of the list depending on (again) default settings

In that box are the exact degrees of every planet.

At the bottom of that box is the degree of the Ascendant, the MC, and the degrees of your 2nd/3rd/11th and 12th houses.

If you've done this correctly all those numbers should be the same degree number as your Ascendant.

The MC will be a different degree.

Again we're not covering the M.C in this book, so ignore it for the moment.

Aspect Graph

Next to that box in the bottom middle of the page is a graph showing little aspect symbols along with the symbols for each planet.

Again, we're not covering those in this book.

Bottom Right Box

The last little box at the bottom of the chart is bottom right

And that has the initials F,A,E,W going down the left of the box and C,F,M along the top.

These initials stand for Fire, Air, Earth, Water and Cardinal, Fixed and Mutable.

So you'll be able to quickly see how many and which of your planets are in those Elements and Qualities/Modes.

Top Left Box

Top left of your chart should have your name and the data you've inputted into astro.com

Your time of birth will be there and will be converted into Universal Time and Sidereal time.

Clock Face

Now, if you imagine your chart is a clock-face, at the quarter to nine/ 8.45am position will be the initials AC and the degree numbers of your Ascendant.

All the signs of the Zodiac will be written on the outside of the circle with Fire signs in Red, Air signs in Yellow, Earth signs in Green and Water signs in Blue.

The sign/symbols will go in order around the circle from Aries-Pisces.

Next are printed each house with black lines dividing the circle up.

Each ones of those lines divides each house from each other.

There are also teeny lines jutting inwards and outwards from each house/sign of the Zodiac

Each one of those is a segments of degrees, with a slightly longer line for every 5th degree.

There are 6 of those in total for each sign of the Zodiac

5 x 6 = 30 30 x 12 = 360

Now, the house division lines might not match-up with the signs of the Zodiac on the outside of the circle.

That's perfectly 'normal'.

If your Asc is 1 degree or less or 29 degrees or more, you might find it harder to see where one house ends and another begins.

Just remember that whatever your Asc sign is, the 7th house will be the 7th sign from your Asc (when you're counting include your Asc sign as number 1)

I've put some chart examples here:

And here:

For what those types of charts look like.

You'll need to know what sign each house STARTS in, to do the chart ruler work in Chapter Six.

Planets in Houses

Then all of your planets are shown in each house as a Planetary symbol.

Some of them might have a little r for retrograde next to them.

And the degree numbers will be rounded-up for the purposes of your chart's picture, so always check the exact numbers on the box bottom left.

In the dead centre of the chart (should be) a circle.

That 'represents' the Earth on which we live.

If you imagine that the horizontal line going from the AC across the chart and out the other side of that circle, is the real horizon, then you'll see some planets are below the horizon and some might be above.

If you were born during day-light the Sun will be above that horizontal/horizon line.

So always eye-ball a chart when you make it to be sure that you've inputted the correct time-of-day.

Someone born at 11pm will have their Sun sign symbol below that horizon regardless on where in the world they were born.

EVERY country in the world has a day-time and a night time

I only mention this as an early student of mine was born in Australia and she got confused with her chart while living in England and thought she'd have to reverse her chart now she was living here.

We soon cleared up that mistake which didn't become apparent until she'd started on her third lesson.

Your birth chart relates to the actual location of the actual planets on the day you were born.

Position of the Moon

Another problem can be people see their Moon in their chart as being above the horizon and think:

'That's wrong, I was born during the day, how can the Moon show above the horizon in my chart?'

This was a real issue with someone until I explained the Moon can be visible during the day, it doesn't only come out at night!

The other thing to understand is you won't be able to actually see all the planets in your chart on your birthday as some need telescopes to be visible.

We just have to rely on data-input from astronomers and astrologers to planetary locations.

And the 'view' of a chart is as if you were in space yourself looking at the Earth and the planets around the Earth.

Some will be more distant, like Pluto and some will be easily visible from outer space such as the Moon (which orbits around the Earth)

Remember Astrology was invented before telescopes, before calculators, before the written word.

Our Solar System

Now we know that the planets all orbit around the Sun, not that they orbit around us.

The principles are the same though.

Plotting the position of the parts of the Solar System we live in and making some sense of what might appear to be random placements.

Planets Near House Lines

Now, you should be able to see which of your planets are in which house.

It makes NO difference if a planet is very near to the line of a house.

Some computer programmes (which really winds me up) will interpret a planet near a house line as being in the house on the other side of the line.

Which is to me a daft idea.

A planet is in a house in that sign no matter what the degree is.

If you Asc was 29 degrees, each house would start at 29 degrees.

If you have a planet that is 29 degrees it will be in that house UNLESS the minutes are MORE than the degree of your Asc.

(I'm only mentioning this for Virgo readers as if you're a Gemini you're unlikely to want to bother with these minor details !!)

Don't rely on 'looking' at the chart to find things out, double-check the degrees.

Why?

Because there is a big difference between something like Sun-in-the-4th-house and Sun-in-the-5th-house.

Now none of these worries will be yours if you don't have an accurate birth **time.**

If you're born in England or Wales, unless you've got a written record of your birth time (rather than your mother's memory) your Asc degree and the house degrees won't be truly accurate....so keep that in mind when you're interpreting planets-in-houses.

All you can do in that case, is read up on planets in SIGNS.

And the aspects between one planet and another.

I'm assuming for the purposes of this book that you have an accurate birth time.

Let's go through the houses in your chart and I'll cover the 'problems' that might arise while you're looking and your chart.

Two or More Planets in Different Signs in One House

If you have two or more planets in one house and they're in different signs, it doesn't matter.

You still read the interpretation for the planet-in-the-sign-in-the-house.

Now, they could also be conjunct to each other.

How would that work?

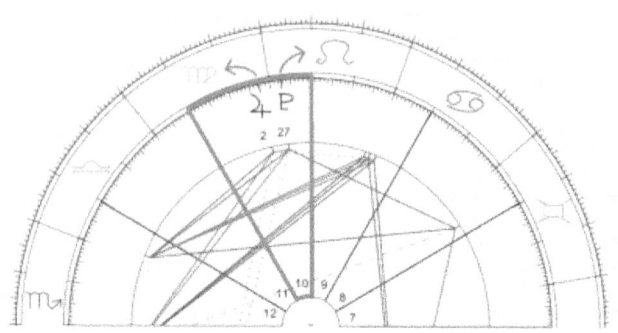

Pod Cast Person: Jupiter in Virgo, Pluto in Leo in 10th house

In our chart example for Podcast Person they have Jupiter in Virgo and Pluto in Leo in the 10th house.

Using our keywords we can say:

You are perfectly (Virgo) lucky (Jupiter) & want to lavish (Leo) deep change (Pluto) in your career (10th house)

Two or More Planets in the Same sign in One House

This is more likely to be the case if you're born with an Indigo birth chart.

See my book ***The Astrology of Indigos*** for more info.

If those planets are all closely linked = less than 8 degrees between each one, then they're called a Stellium.

More info about that in my podcast here Stellium podcast link: https://astromary.libsyn.com/episode-112

A cluster of planets or a stellium will affect how each planet operates.

Think of it like parking in a car park or parking lot and someone has parked their car right up next to yours.

It'll make it very difficult for you to move your car, you'll risk bashing the car next to you, so you have less room to manoeuvre and can only drive straight out of the space.

If the car next to you actually touches your car, if/when you decide to move, you might take their wing mirror or door with you! And if you're *really* unlucky and they've left their hand-brake off, you could move your car and their car will be dragged along with yours.

So the only way to deal with the situation is for you and the car next to you, to leave the space at the same time. Regardless of the type of car or driver. You'll both have to carefully exit straight ahead.

Tight conjunctions and clustered planets mean the planets operate as a sort of gang, rather than separate entities.

It's not a problem, it's just the way things are.

Use your planetary key-words and stick them all together.

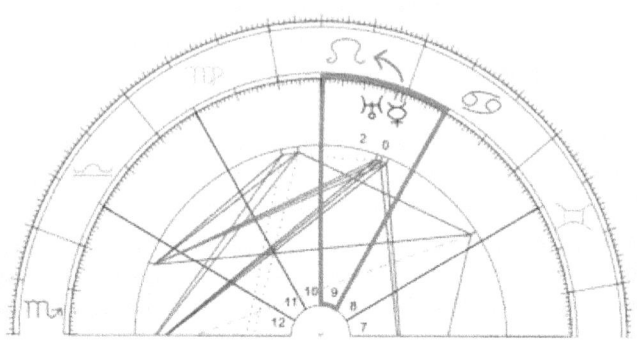

Pod Cast Person: Mercury in Leo conjunct Uranus in Leo

In our Podcast Person's chart we have Mercury in Leo very close to Uranus in Leo. Only 2 degrees apart, so this is a very strong conjunction.

We could say

You lavish (Leo) your thoughts (Mercury) about your philosophies (9th house) with sudden happenings (Uranus)

Another meaning would be this person has and erratic way of thinking and wants to be inspired with the depth of knowledge in the world.

Now keep in mind I can explain things from my perspective, and that might not resonate with your experience.

Even though you might have some planets in the same signs and houses as someone else, until you're their Astro duplicate your lives will always differ.

Astrology allows us to demonstrate our differences so we learn that we're all unique beings.

Lush!

Planets right next to the house line

Sometimes you can have a planet that's right next to the line of the house.

On the chart picture it will look as if it's in one house, when actually it's in the next house.

This goes back to having exact degrees and checking numbers.

Having an Asc that's 0 degrees

It would be very rare to have an Asc that was exactly 0 degrees and no minutes or seconds.

Not impossible, but more rare.

If that were the case, then each of your other houses would once again start at 0 degrees.

It's really not an issue and if this is your chart, congratulations, your chart will be easier to look at!

The Degree of the Asc v.s. the Degree of the MC

In the Equal house system these two points won't relate to each other because the Midheaven is a point of the ecliptic.

At around 12pm local time, the Sun will be in its highest point in the sky.

And it's not something that is always directly over-head because of the tilt of the Earth and our obit and also where you're born in the world and what time of year it is.

The Sun looks "lower" in the sky in Winter in the UK than it does in Summer.

This bit of the sky is called the MC taken from the Latin *Medium Coeli* or as Astrologers call it : The Midheaven

It's an important point if you're using the Placidus system because it is where the 10th house starts.

Unlike all the houses which will start with the same degree, the MC and ASC won't be the same degree.

In the Equal House system the MC can be located in any house from the 8th to the 11th.

However, it won't normally be more or less than 90 degrees from the Ascendant.

Is there a difference between which house the MC is located in?

Yes.

But that's for another book!

I hope you have enjoyed learning a little about the Equal House system.

You can find me at www.maryenglish.com

May Your Astro Journey be Blessed:) xx

End Notes

Down's Syndrome: the spelling in the UK has the apostrophe & the 's' as it was named after the British doctor John Langdon Down who described the syndrome in 1866. In the USA it's spelt without the 's'.

Jargon Buster

There are a lot of older terms and words in Astrology and I've collected some of them here so you can check them if you come across them and aren't sure what they mean.

I have endeavoured in this book to keep things in easy English. But sometimes I have to use an Astrological term as it's a sort of shorthand.

Aspect

The mathematical relationships between one planet and another, shown in a chart as coloured lines between each planet. Or in the graph as little symbols. The main ones are: Conjunction, Sextile, Square, Trine and Inconjunct. There are lots of others if you want to delve deeper.

Elements

There are 4 elements: Fire, Air, Earth & Water.

The Fire signs are: Aries, Leo & Sagittarius.

The Air signs are: Gemini, Libra & Aquarius

The Earth signs are: Taurus, Virgo & Capricorn

The Water signs are: Cancer, Scorpio & Pisces

M.C

Astrologers call this the Midheaven and it's from the Latin 'Medium Coeli'

Quality Or Modality

The signs can be divided into Cardinal, Mutable & Fixed

The Cardinal signs are Aries, Cancer, Libra & Capricorn

The Mutable signs are Gemini, Virgo, Sagittarius & Pisces

The Fixed signs are Taurus, Scorpio & Aquarius

Retrograde

Planets can go retrograde. All of them except the Sun & Moon. At certain times of the year, it looks to us on Earth as if they're going backwards in their Zodiac path. This is because they're moving at different speeds to us in their orbits around the Sun. They're not actually going backwards, it's an optical illusion. Astrologers consider a retrograde planet to operate in a different way to one that is 'direct'.

Transit

One planet moving (literally) through the sky at any given time. Transits can be plotted in the past, present and future. A bit like traffic passing you on the motorway.

References

1. p54 Astrology From Ancient Babylon to the Present, P.G. Maxwell-Stuart, 2012, Amberley Publishing, Stroud, Gloucestershire, GL5 4EP

2. page 183, The Dawn of Astrology, *A Cultural History of Western Astrology,* Volume 1: The Ancient and Classical Worlds, Nicholas Campion, 2008, Continuum Books, London SE1 7NX

3. p46 The New Waite's Compendium of Natal Astrology with Ephemeris for 1880-1980 and Universal Table of Houses, Colin Evans, 1967, Routledge and Kegan Paul Ltd

4. https://www.astro.com/astrowiki/de/Giovanni_Antonio_Magini

5. Flagellum Placideanum or a Whip for Placidianism, GOSPORT, printed by James Phillpott, at the upper end of Middle-Street, 1711. Held at the British Library scanned and accessed via Google Books 18th July 2022 : https://www.google.co.uk/books/edition/_/6RhbAAAAcAAJ?hl=en&gbpv=1&pg=PP1

Bibliography

The Modern Text Book of Astrology, revised edition, Margaret E.Hone, reprinted November 1980, L.N. Fowler & Co. Ltd, 1201/3 High Road, Chadwell Health, Romford, Essex, RM6 4DH

The Astrologers and Their Creed, Christopher McIntosh, 1971, Arrow Books, London W1

Astrology, The Stars and Human Life: A Modern Guide, Christopher McIntosh, 1970, Macdonald Unit 75, London W1

The Equal Houses, Beth Koch, 1991, American Federation of Astrologers, PO Box 22040, Arizona 85285-2040

The Only Way to Learn Astrology, Volume III, Horoscope Analysis, Marion March & Joan McEvers, 1982, ACS Publications, CA 92116

Zodiac, Writer, Astrologer, John Hare, AptecSoft Limited 1997

Don't miss out!

Visit the website below and you can sign up to receive emails whenever Mary English publishes a new book. There's no charge and no obligation.

https://books2read.com/r/B-A-WODI-UAKGC

BOOKS 2 READ

Connecting independent readers to independent writers.

Did you love *Enjoying Equal House, Why One of the Oldest Astrological House Systems is so Easy to Use*? Then you should read *The Astrology of Lovers, How Astrology Can Help You Love Better*[1] by Mary English!

[2]

Single and Looking for Love?

Not sure if the one you're with is the Right One?

Need answers to Love Questions?

If you would like gentle, relevant guidance on your love life then look no further The Astrology Of Lovers.

Using real life examples and cases from her extensive files, Astrologer **Mary English** reveals how to make your relationship easier and more fulfilling.

---

1. https://books2read.com/u/bwqBGY

2. https://books2read.com/u/bwqBGY

Including the Astrology charts from the poets Elizabeth Barrett Browning and her husband Robert, musician John Lennon and his wife artist Yoko Ono.

You will learn how Astrology works, what makes it the ideal way to discover your inner Love Secrets and how it will help you Love Better.

Read more at https://www.maryenglish.com.

Also by Mary English

The Astrology of Lovers, How Astrology Can Help You Love Better
The Astrology of Indigos, Everyday Solutions to Spiritual Difficulties
Neptune in Pisces, An Astrological Search for Enlightenment
Enjoying Equal House, Why One of the Oldest Astrological House Systems is so Easy to Use

Watch for more at https://www.maryenglish.com.

About the Author

Mary English is an experienced author, astrologer, homeopath, and hypnotherapist. Born in London and educated in Switzerland, Mary comes from a large family and is one of five children. With over 20 years of experience in alternative therapies, Mary's mission is to empower her clients and readers to take control of their health and wellbeing.

Mary is the host of the popular FREE weekly podcast, 'Learn Astrology with Mary,' available on all major platforms. Her expertise in astrology also led her to become a resident astrologer for several prominent publications and radio shows, including 'The Green Parent' magazine and BBC Radio Somerset. Mary has also been a guest on Talk Radio Europe, Spain's largest English language radio network.

She lives and works in Bath U.K.

Her books include: *The Astrology of Indigos; Everyday Solutions to Spiritual Difficulties, Neptune in Pisces An Astrological Search for Enlightenment* and *The Astrology of Lovers; How Astrology Can Help You Love Better.*

A Little at a Time, Homeopathy For You and Those You Love published by John Hunt Publishing

Mary is also the author of 12 Sun sign books: *How to Survive a Pisces, How to Bond with an Aquarius, How to Cheer up a Capricorn,*

How to Believe in a Sagittarius, How to Win the Trust of a Scorpio, How to Love a Libra, How to Soothe a Virgo, How to Lavish a Leo, How to Care for a Cancer, How to Listen to a Gemini, How to Satisfy a Taurus and How to Appreciate an Aries also published by John Hunt Publishing.

She writes a monthly Sun sign column for her Newsletter subscribers.

She is a reformed Pisces.

Read more at https://www.maryenglish.com.

About the Publisher

Future Path Publishing is a small Astrological Publisher based in England.

Milton Keynes UK
Ingram Content Group UK Ltd.
UKHW031440121024
449426UK00013B/722